This journal belongs to

....

Date

....

WHEN A WOMAN PRAYS

JOURNAL

T.D. JAKES

Ellie Claire
Hachette Book Group
1290 Avenue of the Americas, New York, NY 10104
ellieclaire.com

First Edition: Hardcover (September 2021)

Ellie Claire is a division of Hachette Book Group, Inc.
The Ellie Claire name and logo are trademarks of Hachette Book Group, Inc.

Unless otherwise noted, the quotes in this book were taken from T. D. Jakes's book *When Women Pray.*

Print book interior design by Bart Dawson.

ISBN: 9781546013723

Printed in China

RRD-S

10 9 8 7 6 5 4 3 2 1

"So let us come boldly to the throne of our gracious God. There we will receive His mercy, and we will find grace to help us when we need it most."

HEBREWS 4:16 NLT

CONTENTS

INTRODUCTION

*P*rayer is a vital foundation for all who choose to follow God. Indeed, without establishing a direct connection to God through prayer, we cannot follow Him. We will have no idea where He is leading.

And while there have been many great men of prayer as individuals over the course of millennia, it is women in general who have carried the lion's share of that load.

Both today and throughout history, women have been especially powerful in taking up the mantle of prayer. While men of old cut timbers and tilled the ground to build our homesteads and cities, it was largely the prayers of women that established the spiritual sanctuary of our families. As men took up arms to fight the great wars of history, the prayers and petitions of women have regularly stemmed the tide of evil in spiritual battle. And though the majority of leadership positions in our churches are filled by men, it is mostly women who fill our sanctuaries with prayers and shouts of praise that reach the very throne of God.

Not only have I seen in my own life the wonder and the humility of women who pray, I have also benefited from such women—and benefited greatly. I have no doubt I am writing these pages today because of the prayers of the matriarchs who came before me. Whatever success I have experienced in life and ministry has a direct connection to the women who have supported and encouraged me not only through their hard work and sound advice but also through their constant prayers.

Our world is a stressful place in many ways. Life is constantly changing and continually presents new challenges. Yet I look to the future with confidence and joy. Why? Because I serve a great and mighty God. And because I have witnessed with my own eyes all the good that can happen when women pray.

As I look out across cultures and societies today, I see women breaking new ground and blazing new trails in every way imaginable. Women are climbing corporate ladders at rapid speeds and ascending to the highest levels of success. They are running countries, leading with integrity and passion. They are launching businesses and spearheading innovations. They are excelling in the classroom, in the boardroom, and in every room.

Amazingly, women have championed these advances outside the home without sacrificing the precious lives within their homes. Because of changes in both technology and social norms, modern women are balancing work and family in ways that would have seemed impossible to mothers of previous generations. They are marrying wonderful men of God and partnering to raise gifted children who in their turn will bless the world anew.

Praise God!

Still, there's a danger that in our march toward progress and prosperity we may leave behind one of the key ingredients to our success. Prayer.

This book is a call for women of all generations to continue their march toward equality and empowerment, yet to do so by once again embracing the power of prayer. This is a call for women in every community to dream like their daughters and pray like their grandmothers.

The world of the future will need women who understand both the power and the protection available only through prayer. We will need women warriors who can raise their swords in the continuing fight against oppression and injustice, and we will need women with shields to defend the innocent and the untrained.

It is only through prayer that such a widespread movement will be sustained. It is only through prayer that these wonderful advances will not only hold but continue forward.

Just as importantly, I want women to remember the wonder of prayer not only as a general principle, but as something vital in their own lives. Prayer is a stress-reliever. It's a chain-breaker. It's a peace-bringer, and it's necessary for every child of God no matter their age or experience.

As Dr. Maya Angelou once said, "I know that when I pray, something wonderful happens. Not just to the person or persons for whom I'm praying, but also something wonderful happens to me. I'm grateful that I'm heard."

That's what I want for you. To be heard. To be sustained. To find the joy and the peace and the confidence your Creator intended you to receive from Him long before the foundations of the earth were set down.

In the pages that follow, you will find stories of women who lived out these truths. Specifically, you will find ten women of the Bible whose propensity to pray in all circumstances set them apart as shining examples in the darkness of the ancient world.

As you read, I pray the light reflected by these women will both illuminate your mind and inspire your heart to follow in their example. I pray you will know the depth of insight, the breadth of compassion, and the height of worship all women can experience when they actively and intentionally bend their knees to pray.

HOW TO USE THIS JOURNAL

This journal has been designed as a companion to *When Women Pray*. It's meant to provide a space for you to reflect on the powerful principles you're exploring and put them into practice in your own prayer life.

Each of the forty days includes key quotes from the original book, as well questions to consider and additional quotes and Scriptures to inspire you as you pray.

There are a number of ways to use the blank space in these pages:

- Write your prayers as letters to God, just as you might write to a friend. You could even begin, "Dear God" or "Dear Jesus," and sign your name at the end.
- Start with a few personal reflections or responses to the reading, and then transition into prayer at the end.
- Make lists of specific prayer needs or concerns. (You may want to leave space to come back later and record how and when these prayers were answered.)
- Some days, instead of writing, you might want to draw or paint or create a collage by pasting pictures that visually represent who or what you are praying for, or what you believe God is saying to you.

There's no right or wrong way. This is your journal. Make it your own. No two women will pray exactly the same way. No two women will have the same journey or the same kind of prayer life. It's as individual to each of us as is our relationship with God.

Speaking of which, this journal is arranged as a forty-day journey of prayer—because forty days is a significant number in Scripture (for example, Jesus Himself fasted and prayed for forty days) and because it's a great length of time to devote to establishing a new habit or discipline or to commit to a special focus or priority in your life. If you follow the forty-day format, you will spend four days praying through the principles found in each chapter of the original book.

However, you should not feel pressured to rush through either the book or the journal. Take as much time as you need. Let God lead. Embrace the adventure and discover for yourself what happens when women pray.

"Dear Jesus, help us to spread Your fragrance everywhere
we go. Flood our souls with Your Spirit and Life.
Penetrate and possess our whole being so utterly that
our lives may only be a radiance of Yours.
Shine through us and be so in us that every soul
we come in contact with may feel Your presence in our souls.
Let them look up and see no longer us, but only Jesus!"

MOTHER TERESA

CHAPTER ONE

Hannah

"Hannah was in deep anguish, crying bitterly
as she prayed to the Lord. And she made this vow:
'O Lord of Heaven's Armies, if you will look upon
my sorrow and answer my prayer and give me a son,
then I will give him back to You.
He will be Yours for his entire lifetime...'"

1 SAMUEL 1:10–11 NLT

When women pray,
God brings about
new life.

DAY 1

*W*hatever your specific desire may be, we all carry the burden of unfulfilled longings. We all feel the burden and the void of dreams yet to come true. Take a moment to think about your unfulfilled longings—those dreams and desires you've carried for what seems like a lifetime.

Are you talking to God about them? Have you asked God to receive them? If so, keep asking. He hears you. He has not forgotten you. If you have not been asking God to receive those longings, there is no better time than the present.

"All my longings lie open before you, Lord;
my sighing is not hidden from you." PSALM 38:9 NIV

"Blessed is she who has believed that the Lord would fulfill
His promises to her!" LUKE 1:45 NIV

DAY 2

*D*o you realize that God often intentionally brings rivals into your life to provoke you? Not to provoke you to anger or jealousy, but to provoke you toward greatness. To poke you and prod you toward the potential He sees in you. When you encounter those who look better, do better, have better, love better, wear better, drive better—whatever the "better" is—you need to understand there is a real possibility God is using that provocation to point you toward Himself so that He can bless you in the same way.

Who or what is God using in your life to provoke you? How have you responded? Ask God to open your eyes to what He is doing in your heart and life today.

"Turn your wounds into wisdom." OPRAH WINFREY

"And let us consider one another to provoke unto love
and to good works." HEBREWS 10:24 KJV

DAY 3

There are two basic choices we can make when we respond to provocation. The first choice is to get jealous, to become envious. The second choice you can make when you are provoked by a rival is to pray. Specifically, you can recognize that if God chose to birth a blessing in your rival's life, then He has the power to birth that same blessing—or an even greater blessing—in you. Which means you should turn to Him in prayer and ask for that blessing rather than lay hands on what has already been given to someone else. Ask Him now.

"You do not have because you do not ask God." JAMES 4:2 NIV

"Keep on asking, and you will receive what you ask for.
Keep on seeking, and you will find. Keep on knocking,
and the door will be opened to you." MATTHEW 7:7 NLT

DAY 4

Whenever you approach the throne of God, be yourself. When you come before God in prayer, come as you are. Stop worrying about your image, and stop worrying about what you look like or what people might think about you. You don't need fancy words. You don't need to clean yourself up or find a preacher to pray on your behalf. Simply come to God as you are—and ask.

Fall on your knees before God with passion and fervency, and He will open the windows of heaven and pour out a blessing you won't have room enough to receive!

There are no magic words in prayer. There is only the grace of God.

You can't twist God's arm and make Him do what you want;
you can only kneel at His feet, pour out your heart, and believe
He will answer—and that His answer will be for your benefit.

CHAPTER TWO

Mary

"My soul glorifies the Lord and my spirit rejoices in God
my Savior, for He has been mindful of the humble state of His
servant. From now on all generations will call me blessed,
for the Mighty One has done great things
for me—holy is His name."

LUKE 1:46–49 NIV

When women pray,
God brings redemption
and reconciliation
into darkness.

DAY 5

*L*et me say something you may need to hear, even if you find it difficult to believe: you are highly favored. If you have received any kind of blessing and provision in your life, then you are highly favored. Why? Because you did nothing to earn or deserve those blessings. You are a recipient of God's grace.

Mary responded to God's grace in her life by declaring a prayer of praise. She did not glorify God merely with her lips, but all the way down to her soul. She praised the Lord from her innermost being because she understood she had been blessed. May the same be true of you and me, because we are highly favored.

Take a few moments to count some of the many ways you have been blessed—the evidence that you are highly favored. Or let Mary's prayer inspire you to write your own prayer of praise.

"Let all that I am praise the Lord; with my whole heart,
I will praise His holy name." PSALM 103:1 NLT

"Glory to God in the highest heaven and on earth peace to those on whom His favor rests." LUKE 2:14 NIV

DAY 6

Mary prophesied that Jesus would bring light into the darkness of the world. And not just her world, but ours as well. What are some ways you have experienced the darkness of this world? How are you experiencing darkness right now? Right this very moment?

Share your thoughts and feelings about this darkness with God in prayer.

"For it is you who light my lamp; the Lord God lightens my darkness."

PSALM 18:28 ESV

"He brought them out of darkness, the utter darkness,
and broke away their chains." PSALM 107:14 NIV

DAY 7

When you are surrounded by a darkness that threatens to overwhelm your very soul, your only hope is prayer. Your only source of relief is to remember that darkness is never stronger than light. And you have access to the Light when you turn to Him in prayer.

Whatever your circumstances may be, pray for Light.

"I am the light of the world. Whoever follows Me will never walk in darkness, but will have the light of life." JOHN 8:12 NIV

"The morning light from heaven is about to break upon us, to give light
to those who sit in darkness and in the shadow of death,
and to guide us to the path of peace." LUKE 1:78-79 NLT

DAY 8

*M*ary's faithfulness to pray—and to respond to what God communicated to her in prayer—resulted in the incredible gift of eternal life offered to all who would receive it. That's because the final result of Mary's prayers was the birth, life, death, and resurrection of Jesus Christ. Jesus has redeemed us. He canceled the debt of our slavery to sin and purchased our freedom at the cost of His own life.

Have you tasted that freedom? Do you want more life in your life? Do you want more light in your darkness? Do you want to see relationships healed and the very armies of heaven sent down to work on your behalf?

Then pray.

"In Him we have redemption through his blood, the forgiveness of sins,
in accordance with the riches of God's grace." EPHESIANS 1:7 NIV

When you see no hope for reconciliation in your broken relationships, your best hope is to pray. God is capable of making momentous things happen in order to restore what has been lost.

Use this space to express creatively what God's grace means to you.

CHAPTER THREE

Sarah

"And by faith even Sarah, who was past childbearing age,
was enabled to bear children because she considered Him
faithful who had made the promise."

HEBREWS 11:11 NIV

When women pray,
they find hope and joy
in unexpected places.

DAY 9

Sometimes God hears the secret whispers of our hearts even when those whispers never escape our lips. Remember that God is omniscient—He knows all things, up to and including the thoughts in our minds and the longings in our hearts. And there are times God chooses to act based on those thoughts or longings without any official request from us.

Aren't you grateful that's true? Aren't you grateful God knows you better than you know yourself? Aren't you grateful that God's Spirit living inside you understands exactly what you need even when you are unable to articulate that need in a way that makes sense?

Take a few moments to think of some prayers you didn't know to pray—but God answered anyway. Thank Him for knowing and understanding the deepest longings of your heart today.

"You have searched me, Lord, and you know me." PSALM 139:1 NIV

"In the same way the Spirit [comes to us and] helps us in our weakness. We do not know what prayer to offer or how to offer it as we should, but the Spirit Himself [knows our need and at the right time] intercedes on our behalf with sighs and groanings too deep for words." ROMANS 8:26 AMP

DAY 10

*E*ach of us receives specific promises from God that are unique to us as individuals. These are promises spoken directly to our spirits—truths we hear and incorporate into our lives without really understanding how or why they arrived. They are God-given guarantees of what He will accomplish if we choose to believe them and choose to respond in faith.

In addition, Scripture is filled with many universal promises that apply to all who have received salvation through faith in Jesus Christ.

What are God's promises to you today?

"Therefore I tell you, whatever you ask for in prayer, believe that you have received it, and it will be yours" MARK 11:24 NIV

"My God will meet all your needs according to the riches
of His glory in Christ Jesus" PHILIPPIANS 4:19 NIV

DAY 11

God knows you. God values you. God sees you in the midst of your circumstances, and He wants you to know His promises are true for you. The blessings He has promised apply to you, and they are coming for you.

How do you respond to God's promises when you encounter them? What happens inside you when you read or remember them?

Ask God to give you faith to believe in the fulfillment of His promises today.

"Whatever God has promised gets stamped with the Yes of Jesus.
In Him, this is what we preach and pray, the great Amen, God's Yes
and our Yes together, gloriously evident. God affirms us, making us
a sure thing in Christ, putting His Yes within us. By His Spirit He has
stamped us with His eternal pledge—a sure beginning of what
He is destined to complete." 2 CORINTHIANS 1:20-22 MSG

"Gather the riches of God's promises. Nobody can take away from you those texts from the Bible which you have learned by heart." CORRIE TEN BOOM

DAY 12

Waiting for God to fulfill His promises can be difficult. Like you, I have felt the weight of waiting. The burden. It piles up day after day, year after year, until it begins to feel unbearable. Unmanageable. But we can bear the weight when our waiting is matched with prayer. We can manage the years when our waiting is supported and uplifted by prayer—by a continued communication with the God who gave us the promise in the first place.

You'll never make it in your own strength, but you don't have to. You can choose to pray and submit yourself to God's timing. You can trust Him to make good when it will produce the most good.

Offer God this season of waiting in a prayer of faith and trust.

"And we know that in all things God works for the good of those who
love Him, who have been called according to His purpose" ROMANS 8:28 NIV

"I wait for the Lord, my whole being waits, and in His word
I put my hope." PSALM 130:5 NIV

CHAPTER FOUR

The Woman with the Issue of Blood

"Daughter, your faith has healed you.
Go in peace and be freed from your suffering."

MARK 5:34 NIV

When women pray,
they gain victory over
the "issues" of life.

DAY 13

We're all dealing with issues. Every one of us. We're all dealing with pain. We're all dealing with problems that threaten to overwhelm us. We're all dealing with difficult circumstances that will try to define who we are—if we allow them.

What issues are you facing today? What's your biggest issue? How have you tried to resolve it in the past? What are you asking God to do?

_____

_____

_____

_____

_____

_____

_____

_____

_____

_____

_____

_____

_____

_____

_____

_____

_____

When your issue threatens to swallow up even your name,
your only hope is prayer.

"Lord, hear my prayer, listen to my cry for mercy; in your faithfulness and righteousness come to my relief." PSALM 143:1 NIV

DAY 14

When you are in danger of being swallowed up or defined by your issues, don't complain about it. Don't let yourself get down in the dumps. Grab hold of God! Grab Him and don't let go.

Imagine, like the woman in Scripture, you have caught hold of the hem of His garment. Jesus has just asked, "Who touched me?" He's looking at you. Look back into His eyes of love and answer Him.

Pour out your heart to Him in prayer.

"I will not let you go unless you bless me." GENESIS 32:26 NIV

"I press on to take hold of that for which Christ Jesus
took hold of me." PHILIPPIANS 3:12 NIV

DAY 15

ake no mistake: this world will always try to convince you that you're not enough. Not only that, but we have a spiritual enemy in this world, and he will work overtime to make you believe you're not enough.

Don't let any of it work. Don't believe a word of it. Because the overwhelming message of God's revelation through the Scripture is that you are more than enough.

Tell God what it means to you to know this. Ask Him to help you believe it in the very depths of your being:

"I have loved you, my people, with an everlasting love.
With unfailing love I have drawn you to myself." JEREMIAH 31:3 NLT

You are the apple of God's eye. You are His treasured possession.
You are cherished. Loved. Sought out. Chosen. You are worth searching for
and fighting for. You are worth dying for! You are valuable to God.
Never allow anything to prevent you from coming to Him in prayer.

DAY 16

My sister, you and I both know there is an "issue" dragging you down. It's been there a long time. It's been pulling on you a long time. I don't know what it is, but you do. I don't know what caused it, but you do. I don't know everything you've done to try to remove it or get yourself out from under it in some way, but you know. You're desperate for answers.

Do not stop reaching until you've grabbed hold of God. Don't stop stretching until you touch your Savior—He's waiting for you. He's hesitating in that crowd, slowing down right in front of you. Don't stop praying until you hear His voice, because you know what He will say when He looks down and sees the tears streaking down your face: "Daughter, your faith has healed you."

Keep praying.

Don't stop. Don't give up. Keep going forward. No matter how desperate
your circumstances may seem right now, there is relief in your future.
There is hope in your future. There is healing.

"For the Lord takes delight in His people; He crowns the humble with victory." PSALM 149:4 NIV

CHAPTER FIVE

Naomi

"Then the women of the town said to Naomi, 'Praise the Lord, who has now provided a redeemer for your family!'"

RUTH 4:14 NLT

When women pray,
curses are turned
into blessings.

DAY 17

We all understand that difficult circumstances are part of life. But sometimes the depth and the breadth of those circumstances go way beyond our expectations. Sometimes what we view as a difficult moment can stretch into a season. Not just a struggle, but a season of struggle. Not just a single trial or tragedy, but a season of trials and tragedies. A season of suffering.

In these seasons when it seems like everything that can go wrong does go wrong, it's easy to believe life will never be the same. It's easy to believe God has forgotten about you. It's easy to believe you've come under a curse and will never recover.

Winston Churchill said, "If you're going through hell—keep going." That's good advice, but I would change it a little to this: "If you're going through hell, keep praying." Because prayer is what will get you through.

Take a few moments to reflect on the season you find yourself in and commit it to God in prayer.

"My comfort in my suffering is this:
Your promise preserves my life." PSALM 119:50 NIV

"The Lord will fulfill his purpose for me." PSALM 138:8 ESV

DAY 18

*I*f you have any connection with God whatsoever, then the devil is your enemy. And he is relentless in his desire for your destruction. I use that word intentionally. He's not out to mess with you. He doesn't want to disturb you. He doesn't care about disrupting you. He wants to destroy you.

There's bad news and good news when it comes to Satan's influence in our lives. The bad news is that he is stronger than you. Stronger than me. Stronger than any of us.

When you face an enemy stronger than you and smarter than you, your only hope is to pray. Because Satan is not stronger than God. In fact, Satan remains directly under the authority of God. That's the good news. You and I have the opportunity to be in direct communication with the One who has already conquered our enemy.

There is power in prayer.

"The One who is in you is greater than the one who is
in the world." 1 JOHN 4:4 NIV

"The thief comes only to steal and kill and destroy; I have come that they may have life, and have it to the full." JOHN 10:10 NIV

DAY 19

*B*itterness is like a root in that it grows deep, down in the places we can't easily see or access. Bitterness has a way of sucking up our hurt and our regret and our sorrow—all the destructive feelings we swim in during seasons of suffering—and then pumping them directly into our hearts. It changes us, withering our hearts and minds from the inside out.

It's bitterness that drives you to feel irritated or even angry at the good fortunes of those around you. It's bitterness that drives you to alcohol or drugs or food or pornography or anything else as a method of coping with your season of suffering. It's bitterness that drives you to blame others for the pain you've experienced—and especially to blame God. Instead, when we find ourselves in the midst of suffering, we need to fall down on our knees before God's throne and cry out, "Lord Jesus, have mercy on me, a sinner."

Ask God to show you any "root of bitterness" in your heart. Confess it to Him and receive His forgiveness.

"Watch out that no poisonous root of bitterness grows up to trouble you." HEBREWS 12:15 NLT

"If we [freely] admit that we have sinned and confess our sins,
He is faithful and just [true to His own nature and promises],
and will forgive our sins and cleanse us continually from all
unrighteousness [our wrongdoing, everything not in conformity
with His will and purpose]." 1 JOHN 1:9 AMP

DAY 20

*I*f you read only the first chapter of Ruth, it seems like a depressing story, a disheartening story of an old woman so beaten down by life that she literally gets to the end of her road and gives up. Thankfully, there are three more chapters to Naomi's story—and to Ruth's.

If you're in a season of suffering right now, you need to remember there are more chapters in your life as well. You've still got more story in your story! You've still got more life in your life! So don't give up. Don't allow yourself to be consumed by bitterness or filled with regret. There's more to come for you.

You must not let bitterness and grief overwhelm you during seasons of sorrow—because you never know what God has planned for your future. Like Naomi, you may have kings living in you! You may be the instrument God is honing and shaping to be used in just the right way to produce a blessing unlike anything your city or your community has ever seen.

I'll say it again: if you're going through hell, keep going. And keep praying.

"We also glory in our sufferings, because we know that suffering produces perseverance; perseverance, character; and character, hope." ROMANS 5:3-4 NIV

"And I am certain that God, who began the good work within you,
will continue his work until it is finally finished on the day
when Christ Jesus returns." PHILIPPIANS 1:6 NLT

Use this space to express creatively what having faith means to you.

CHAPTER SIX

The Samaritan Woman

"Everyone who drinks this water will be thirsty again, but whoever drinks the water I give them will never thirst. Indeed, the water I give them will become in them a spring of water welling up to eternal life."

JOHN 4:13–14 NIV

When women pray,
they are quenched
of their thirst.

DAY 21

Many of us are experts at hiding in plain sight. People see us. They talk with us. But they have no idea who we are under the surface. They don't know the real us down inside—and we do everything possible to keep it that way. But there is no hiding from God. There are no secrets between yourself and God. God knows. He always knows. He always sees.

So when you come before God in prayer, come honestly. Come openly. Come prepared to acknowledge all the ways you have rebelled against Him and all the times you have been focused on yourself. Because He already knows.

God has already made provision to forgive you. He's already mapped out a special trip specifically to meet you and talk with you—to heal you and save you, if you'll open your heart and accept what He offers. Open your heart to Him in prayer today.

"Have mercy on me, O God, because of your unfailing love. Because of your great compassion, blot out the stain of my sins." PSALM 51:1 NLT

Jesus Himself is a wellspring of life. Jesus Himself is a fountain of
hope and goodness and provision.

DAY 22

My sister, may I submit to you that there is no purer expression of prayer than what the Samaritan woman asked of Jesus?

"Sir, give me this water."

That is the essence of prayer! After all, what is prayer but recognizing our own emptiness and asking God to fill us with what we need?

In short, prayer is simply saying, "Lord, I am thirsty. Please fill me with Yourself."

"As the deer pants for streams of water, so my soul pants for you, my God.
My soul thirsts for God, for the living God." PSALM 42:1–2 NIV

Lord Jesus, please give me Your water so that I never thirst again.

DAY 23

*M*ake no mistake, the devil always has solutions for your thirst. The devil will always show you different ways to get your needs met. But he's a liar. He wants to devour you. His goal is your destruction.

This world is filled with solutions for your thirst. The economy of our culture is built on inflaming every kind of thirst inside you and then selling you false promises to quench those thirsts. Don't believe those promises.

Jesus wanted to show this woman a better way. Himself. The Living Water. And Jesus wants to show you a better way as well. Because He knows you are thirsty.

God knows you are thirsty. He is the Well sitting on a well, and He is able to quench your thirst. He wants to quench your thirst! The question is, will you let Him?

Jesus is the Living Water. He is the Bread of Life. And He will provide
exactly what you need when you reach out to Him in prayer.

"Let anyone who is thirsty come to me and drink.
Whoever believes in me, as Scripture has said, rivers of living water
will flow from within them." JOHN 7:37–38 NIV

DAY 24

We don't know her name, but this woman defined all her life by her thirst became the instrument through which God satisfied the thirsts of others. This woman who came to Jacob's well alone because she had been shunned by her community became a living well herself—a tributary of God's grace overflowing with life-giving water to that same community.

That's why I want to see millions of women praying in their cities and their towns across the world today. Because when women pray, they are quenched of their thirst—and they open up God's springs of blessing so that entire communities are quenched as well.

Take some time today to pray specifically for your family, friends, and community.

"Tell them how much the Lord has done for you, and how He has had mercy on you." MARK 5:19 NIV

"We no longer believe just because of what you said; now we have
heard for ourselves, and we know that this man really is
the Savior of the world." JOHN 4:42 NIV

CHAPTER SEVEN

Esther

"And who knows but that you have come to your
royal position for such a time as this?"

ESTHER 4:14 NIV

When women pray,
they gain victory
over injustice.

DAY 25

*N*o matter where you look on this planet, there are people who have been defined for generations by their hatred of other people. Wars have been fought because of ignorance and prejudice. Nations and economies have been built through the plunder and exploitation of other nations and economies. Even in societies where people of all races are encouraged to live freely and respect one another, the fractures and fault lines of past failures still run deep—and still rumble more often than we like to admit.

None of these problems can be solved overnight. The world requires healing, and it takes generations to heal from generational damage. It takes the healing power of prayer.

_____

_____

_____

_____

_____

_____

_____

_____

_____

_____

_____

_____

_____

_____

_____

_____

_____

_____

_____

_____

_____

_____

"Confess your sins to each other and pray for each other
so that you may be healed." JAMES 5:16 NLT

"If My people, who are called by My name, will humble themselves
and pray and seek My face and turn from their wicked ways,
then I will hear from heaven, and I will forgive their sin
and will heal their land." 2 CHRONICLES 7:14 NIV

DAY 26

When God opens the windows of heaven and pours out a blessing on you, there's always a reason why. God loves you and genuinely desires your happiness, but there's always more involved with His blessings than simply filling your bank account or blowing up your social media.

God-given blessings include God-assigned responsibility. He has a purpose in mind. He's given you something so that you can make use of it for His glory, not for your own. In other words, you have been blessed so you can be a blessing. You have been extended favor so you can reflect that same favor on others.

Thank God for the favor and blessing in your life and ask Him to show you how He wants you to use it for the benefit of others.

"Great gifts mean great responsibilities; greater gifts, greater responsibilities!" LUKE 12:48 MSG

We need women who are willing to stand up for what they believe in,
not only with words but with action.

DAY 27

I love Esther's plan because it offered a one-two punch against the enemies of her people. The first punch was prayer. That's the left-handed jab in our spiritual warfare. It keeps the enemy off guard. Her second punch was fasting. That's the overhand right—the knockout swing fueled by the Holy Spirit.

Fasting is temporarily abstaining from something physical so you can concentrate on the spiritual. It is removing something of small significance from your life for a time so that you will have extra focus and extra emphasis on that which is eternal.

Consider whether God might be calling you to add fasting to your discipline of prayer. What might that look like? Are you willing—or willing to be made willing—to sacrifice something physical for the sake of the spiritual?

"Is not this the kind of fasting I have chosen: to loose the chains of injustice and untie the cords of the yoke, to set the oppressed free and break every yoke?" ISAIAH 58:6 NIV

DAY 28

*P*rayer works best in community. Spiritual battle is most effective when you've got an army at your back. So when it comes time to roll up your sleeves and fight for the side of good through prayer, first pick up the phone and call your family. Call your friends. Call your neighbors. Call your church. Call your small group or your life group or whatever they call groups in your congregation.

Join with others in fasting and prayer, as Esther did. And then prepare yourself to see the power of God at work, just as Esther saw.

"Trust in Him at all times, you people; pour out your hearts to Him, for God is our refuge." PSALM 62:8 NIV

"When the storm has swept by, the wicked are gone,
but the righteous stand firm forever." PROVERBS 10:25 NIV

Use this space to express creatively what God's strength means to you.

CHAPTER EIGHT

Rhoda

"O Lord, I am Your servant; yes, I am Your servant,
born into Your household; You have freed me from my chains."

PSALM 116:16 NLT

When women pray,
people are set free
from bondage.

DAY 29

God loves regular people—the kinds of people who are typically pushed behind the scenes of society. God not only loves such people, He understands their value. He understands their uniqueness and their unique contributions to this world. Because when ordinary people pray, they gain access to extraordinary power.

Think of ordinary people you know who—through the power of God—have had an extraordinary impact on your life or the lives of others. Ask God to help you follow their example.

....

....

....

....

....

....

....

....

....

....

....

....

....

....

"Remember, dear brothers and sisters, that few of you were wise
in the world's eyes or powerful or wealthy when God called you.
Instead, God chose things the world considers foolish in order to shame
those who think they are wise. And He chose things that are powerless to
shame those who are powerful. God chose things despised by the world,
things counted as nothing at all, and used them to bring to nothing
what the world considers important." 1 CORINTHIANS 1:26-28 NLT

"When God calls you to a great task, He provides you with the strength to accomplish what He has called you to do." CORETTA SCOTT KING

DAY 30

*L*et me ask you: In what ways are you currently living in bondage? When did you first feel the cold harshness of the chains against your wrists, and what were those chains made from?

If you feel locked down and chained up, and you're beginning to lose any hope of freedom, that is a time to pray, because ordinary prayers have extraordinary power to free you from your bondage.

"As a prisoner for the Lord, then, I urge you to live a life worthy of the calling you have received." EPHESIANS 4:1 NIV

"In my distress I prayed to the Lord, and the Lord answered me and set me free." PSALM 118:5 NLT

DAY 31

When you choose to engage with God in prayer, there comes a point early in that process when you need to trust that He is on the case—even if you don't see any evidence of an answer. Perhaps especially when you see no evidence of an answer.

I know there are times when it feels like your prayers have no effect. I know there are moments when it seems like everything you say, everything you pray, is bouncing off the ceiling and falling right back down around your feet.

What I need you to understand is that God is up to something. Even when you can't see what's going on, He's up to something. Even when you don't feel His presence or His power, He's up to something. Even when you've been praying for months or years or even decades and nothing has happened and you are bogged down by doubt and desperation—that is a time to trust Him and keep on praying, because He's up to something.

"Faith is confidence in what we hope for and assurance about
what we do not see." HEBREWS 11:1 NIV

"When you get into a tight place and everything goes against you,
till it seems as though you could not hang on a minute longer,
never give up then, for that is just the place and time
that the tide will turn." HARRIET BEECHER STOWE

DAY 32

There comes a time in the practice of prayer when we need to recognize what God is doing around us. We need to hear the knocking at the door. When that moment comes, we need to switch gears. We need to take off our mourning clothes and put an end to our weeping and feeling sorry for ourselves—because that which we have been praying for is standing at the door!

At some point your prayers will accomplish all they were designed to do, and it will be time for you to act. Open the door!

Ask God to show you where He is at work, where your prayers are already being answered. Thank Him for those answers and take the next steps.

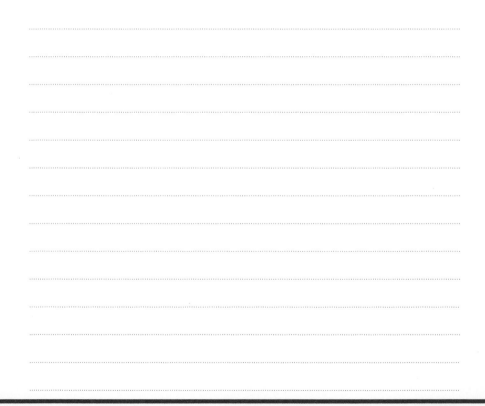

"Let us hold unswervingly to the hope we profess,
for He who promised is faithful." HEBREWS 10:23 NIV

God's extraordinary power will flow through the prayers of ordinary people
when we have the faith to pray—and when we are willing to take action
to open the door and take hold of what God has set before us.

CHAPTER NINE

The Shunamite Woman

"Praise be to the God and Father of our Lord Jesus Christ!
In his great mercy He has given us new birth into
a living hope through the resurrection..."

1 PETER 1:3 NIV

When women pray,
even what is dead
can find life again.

DAY 33

*I*f you want to see God work in your life, you need to make space for Him. If you want to experience God's presence and power, you need to give Him some room to move. Room to breathe.

In the same way, if you want to experience God's blessings—if you want Him to fill you up with what you need and what you desire—you need to make some space. You need to open up an area in which you can receive what you need and what you desire.

How can you make more space for God in your life? Pray about what you can do—or do differently—to open up room for Him to move.

"Here I am! I stand at the door and knock. If anyone hears my voice and opens the door, I will come in." REVELATION 3:20 NIV

God will not try to force His way into your house or your life. He will wait
until you offer Him some space to work, and then He will work.

DAY 34

How often do we try to convince ourselves we don't need anything? How often do we try to convince others that we have it all together? How often do we try to convince God?

One of the reasons you try to deny your longings and your desires is that you've been stung so many times by disappointment. You used to hold out hope; you used to believe and yearn and pray for God to provide that which you desired most to hold. But it never came. The prayers were never answered. And so in order to protect yourself from any further stings—in order to protect yourself from disappointment—you allowed a crust to form over your heart. A hardness. A callousness. A defense mechanism.

Thankfully, God has a way of breaking through that crust. He has a way of breaching our defenses and touching our hearts when He knows the timing is right.

No matter how hard you try, you can't hide your desires from God.
No matter how stridently you deny your own heart, you can't hide
your longings from God. He knows. And He will put His finger on
those desires when you give Him room to do so through prayer.

"Delight yourself in the Lord, and he will give you the desires
of your heart." PSALM 37:4 ESV

DAY 35

How often do we respond to tragedy with stoicism? How often do we try to pretend everything is all right? How often do we try to convince ourselves we don't really need that thing we lost—that person or that dream or that vision or that truth—simply because we lost it?

Take some time today to mourn the tragedies in your life, the dreams that have died, the heartaches and losses. Be honest about how you feel. And ask God to restore your hope.

"My soul is weary with sorrow; strengthen me according to your word." PSALM 119:28 NIV

"Why, my soul, are you downcast? Why so disturbed within me?
Put your hope in God, for I will yet praise Him,
my Savior and my God." PSALM 42:5 NIV

DAY 36

The Shunamite woman made the right choice because she ran toward God—she ran toward His prophet. And when she got within sight of Elijah, she dived onto the ground and took hold of his feet. In other words, this woman was not letting go of God's prophet until God unleashed His power to solve her problem.

Don't deny your needs. Don't deny the pain you feel. Run to God! Grab hold of Him and refuse to let go! Because He is able to bring your dreams to life, even when it sure looks to you and everyone else like they died long ago.

When it feels like your dreams are dying, when it seems like hope itself is slipping through your fingers, run to God and dive at His feet. Grab Him and refuse to let go!

"Though you have made me see troubles, many and bitter, you will restore my life again; from the depths of the earth you will again bring me up." PSALM 71:20 NIV

"I would have despaired had I not believed that I would see the goodness of the Lord in the land of the living." PSALM 27:13 AMP

CHAPTER TEN

Anna

"Coming up to them at that very moment, she gave thanks
to God and spoke about the child to all who were
looking forward to the redemption of Jerusalem."

LUKE 2:38 NIV

When women pray,
people find salvation.

DAY 37

nna recognized her people were in need of a Savior. She was praying for a Savior, not only for herself and her people, but for the world.

What about you? Where do you currently need rescuing? In what areas of life do you feel enslaved or pressed down? Where are you crying out for salvation?

....

....

....

....

....

....

....

....

....

....

....

....

....

....

....

....

When you are a slave to something more powerful than yourself,
you have no hope of escape through your own power. You need a savior.

"Guide me in your truth and teach me, for You are God my Savior, and my hope is in You all day long." PSALM 25:5 NIV

DAY 38

*N*otice the persistence of Anna's prayers. She was dedicated to prayer as the major element of her life. For so many of us, prayer is something we do when we can fit it in, when we can find a little time. That's not how Anna approached life. She never left the temple because prayer was her life. It was her priority. Prayer was the foundation around which she built everything else in her day, her week, her month, and so on.

How about you? How much has prayer been a priority in the past? How has this forty-day journey helped you to be more consistent and persistent in prayer?

"Seek the Lord and his strength; seek his presence continually!"

1 CHRONICLES 16:11 ESV

"Always be joyful. Never stop praying. Be thankful
in all circumstances, for this is God's will for you who belong
to Christ Jesus." 1 THESSALONIANS 5:16-18 NLT

DAY 39

*n*otice the diversity of Anna's prayer life. It's easy to get stuck in ruts in our prayer lives. If we're not careful, we end up doing the same thing over and over, saying the same thing over and over. That's not how Anna prayed.

She was a woman of worship. As she ministered in the temple courts each day, she praised God for His character. She proclaimed His goodness and His faithfulness. She ascribed glory to God, rather than always using prayer as an opportunity to gain something from God.

In addition, Anna incorporated fasting. She chose to regularly forego the temporary pleasure and sustenance of food so that she could plead with God about her great need for salvation. For healing in her life and in the lives of her people. For rescue from the evils around her.

How diverse is your prayer life? Have you found different ways to come to God in a spirit of worship and prayer—to experience His presence?

"Be filled with the Holy Spirit, singing psalms and hymns
and spiritual songs among yourselves, and making music to the Lord
in your hearts. And give thanks for everything to God the Father
in the name of our Lord Jesus Christ." EPHESIANS 5:18-20 NLT

"Before they call I will answer; while they are still speaking
I will hear." ISAIAH 65:24 NIV

DAY 40

Finally, notice the discipline of Anna's prayer life. She prayed on a schedule—"night and day," according to the text. She was intentional about making prayer a priority so that her actions reflected that priority. She had the kind of internal discipline that drives many successful people to order their lives according to what they want, rather than allowing the chaos of life to push them around like boats tossed back and forth by the wind and the waves.

How do you practice the discipline of prayer? How do you make it a priority?

Ask God to show you what can you do going forward, to be intentional about incorporating the power of prayer into your daily life.

"This is the confidence we have in approaching God: that if we ask anything according to His will, He hears us. And if we know that He hears us—whatever we ask—we know that we have what we asked of Him." 1 JOHN 5:14-15 NIV

"Through Jesus, therefore, let us continually offer to God a sacrifice of praise—the fruit of lips that openly profess his name." HEBREWS 13:15 NIV

Whenever you pray,

God will hear you. And He will answer. That's the promise women can rely on when they pray. That's the power women can access when they pray— that connection with Almighty God. That's the wonder and the joy women can experience when they speak with God and then listen for His response, because He does answer.

ABOUT THE AUTHOR

T. D. JAKES—one of the most inspirational, influential, and treasured spiritual leaders of our time—is the #1 *New York Times* bestselling author of more than forty books. He is the CEO of the towering TDJ Enterprises, spanning film, television, radio, publishing, podcasts, and an award-winning music label. He is a Grammy Award–winning music producer, and his blockbuster films have achieved international success at the box office. His inspirational conferences (MegaFest, Woman Thou Art Loosed) continue to have a profound global impact. Bishop Jakes is a master communicator whose trusted voice is heard in more than eighty million homes daily and across a vast worldwide audience via social media. He resides in Dallas, Texas.